# WILLIE McLEAN
### and the
# CIVIL WAR
# SURRENDER

BY CANDICE RANSOM
ILLUSTRATIONS BY JENI REEVES

On My Own
HISTORY

🌾 Carolrhoda Books, Inc./Minneapolis

*To Marty* —*C. R.*

*To the 24th Iowa Volunteer Infantry Regiment* —*J. R.*

Editor's note: The coloration and details of all uniforms in this book, including the blue-gray coat worn by General Robert E. Lee at Appomattox Court House, are based on archival research.

The illustrator wishes to thank Patrick Schroeder, historian at Appomattox Court House National Historical Park, for his valuable knowledge and JPEGs; Mike Dooley for his guidance and loans; and the participants in the annual Civil War reenactment at Usher's Ferry, Cedar Rapids, IA. Special thanks goes to Rosemary Younce and my models: Austin, Hannah, and Tracie Chute, Bryan Davis, and Stuart Reeves.

The photographs on pp. 46–47 appear courtesy of Appomattox Court House National Historical Park.

*This book is available in two editions:*
Library binding by Carolrhoda Books, Inc., a division of Lerner Publishing Group
Soft cover by First Avenue Editions, an imprint of Lerner Publishing Group
241 First Avenue North
Minneapolis, MN 55401 U.S.A.

Website address: www.carolrhodabooks.com


Library of Congress Cataloging-in-Publication Data

Ransom, Candice F., 1952–
    Willie McLean and the Civil War surrender / by Candice Ransom ; illustrations by Jeni Reeves.
        p.    cm. — (On my own history)
    ISBN: 1–57505–588–0 (lib. bdg. : alk. paper)
    ISBN: 1–57505–698–4 (pbk. : alk. paper)
    1. Appomattox Campaign, 1865—Juvenile literature. 2. Lee, Robert E. (Robert Edward), 1807–1870—Juvenile literature. 3. Grant, Ulysses S. (Ulysses Simpson), 1822–1885—Juvenile literature. 4. McLean family—Juvenile literature. 5. Appomattox (Va.)—Biography—Juvenile literature. [1. Appomattox Campaign, 1865. 2. Lee, Robert E. (Robert Edward), 1807–1870. 3. Grant, Ulysses S. (Ulysses Simpson), 1822–1885. 4. United States—History—Civil War, 1861–1865. 5. McLean family.]
    I. Reeves, Jeni, ill. II. Title. III. Series.
    E477.67.R36 2005
    973.7'38—dc22                                                         2003026474

Manufactured in the United States of America
1 2 3 4 5 6 – JR – 10 09 08 07 06 05

# Author's Note

In 1861, America was a divided country. White farmers in the South grew cotton and other crops, using the labor of African American slaves. Others in the South also had slaves. Many Northerners felt that slavery was wrong. The two sides could not agree. The Southern states left the United States, and the Civil War began.

By 1864, Ulysses S. Grant commanded all of the North's soldiers. These troops were called the Union army, or Yankees. Robert E. Lee commanded the South's Confederate army in Virginia.

By April 1865, Grant had driven Lee's troops into the mountains of western Virginia. The armies met near the village of Appomattox Court House. Wilmer McLean and his family lived there in a large brick house on Stage Road.

The McLeans had been touched by the war before. Early in the war, they lived near Bull Run in northern Virginia. During the First Battle of Bull Run, their house was used as Confederate headquarters. A year later, their house was taken over again during the Second Battle of Bull Run. Tired of war, Wilmer McLean moved his family south, where he hoped they would be safe.

Willie McLean was eleven years old in 1865. The McLeans never wrote down what happened that fateful April day, but we know that Willie McLean was present. This is his story, as it might have happened.

*Appomattox Court House, Virginia*

*April 8, 1865*

BOOM!  KABOOM!

Willie McLean jumped off the porch.

Cannons!  The war was here!

"Papa said we can't leave," said Lula.

His seven-year-old sister

hugged her favorite toy,

an old rag doll.

Willie remembered the battles near
their old house in northern Virginia.
He remembered the soldiers in
uniform and the booming guns.
Once a shell from a cannon
had passed through the wall
and into his mother's stewpot.
But since the McLeans had moved here,
the war had always been far away.
This was Willie's chance to see some action.
He ran out of the yard.
"I'm coming with you!" said Lula.
"Go back," he told her.
"I want to see the war!" said Lula.
"Do you have to bring that doll?" said Willie.
He didn't want the soldiers
to think he and Lula were babies.
"Betty goes where I go," Lula said.

A lone horseman led a bony
horse down Stage Road.
He halted when he saw
Willie and Lula.
"Do you have any food?"
he asked.
Willie shook his head.

"Water for my horse?"

asked the man.

"Our well is this way," said Willie.

He drew a bucket from the well house.

"Are you in Lee's army?"

he asked the stranger.

"What's left of it," said the man.

Willie could not believe that
this scarecrow was one of
Robert E. Lee's proud troops.
The man wore a torn shirt
and gray pants with holes.
His battered felt hat was
spattered with mud.
His feet were bare.
"Are you going to fight
in the war?" asked Lula.
The man shook his head.
"I'm sick of war.
Sick of eating parched corn.
Tired of sleeping tied in Tramp's reins
so no one will steal him."
"Where are you going?" asked Lula.
"Home," the man said.
He and Tramp limped down the road.

"Deserter!" Willie said.

"I feel sorry for that man," said Lula.

"He was hungry."

"Real soldiers don't run off,"
Willie said.

"General Lee will beat the Yankees
even if all his men desert."

Willie and Lula kept walking.
Willie didn't see the cannons
he had heard.
But now he could see long lines
of wagons and soldiers
straggling down the road.
Maybe there would be a battle soon!

## Daybreak, April 9

The clatter of hooves woke Willie.

He sprang to the bedroom window.

Hundreds of troopers rode

through the fog like a ghost army.

Lula woke up too.

"What is it?" she whispered,

clutching her doll.

"It must be Lee's cavalry!"

Willie whispered.

"I bet they're gathering for a fight."

He pulled on his pants.

If he hurried,

he could sneak outside.

But he stopped at the top of the stairs.

Candlelight shone

from the parlor below.

Lula crept up behind him,
dragging Betty by one leg.
Downstairs, a man stepped into the hall.
He wore a gray uniform with brass
buttons and high boots.
He must be one of General Lee's officers,
Willie thought.
"Early tomorrow," the officer
said to Willie's father.
"Be sure to protect your family."

"What is he talking about?"
Lula whispered to Willie.
"I bet the battle will be tomorrow morning!"
he answered.
"I'm scared," Lula said.
"Lee's army won't let the Yankees
hurt us," Willie told her.
They went back to bed,
but Willie was too excited to sleep.
In a few hours, he'd be able to watch
the war from his front porch!

*Morning, April 9*

The first guns blasted during breakfast.

Willie's mother screamed.

Lula grabbed her doll

and ducked under the table.

"We'll be all right,"

Willie's father said.

18

The kitchen was the safest
room in the house.
It had been built half underground.
The lower half of the kitchen
was protected by the earth.
If the family stayed low,
bullets wouldn't hurt them.

Willie didn't want to stay low.

He rushed to the window.

Outside he saw galloping horses
and soldiers firing rifles.

Men dropped to the ground.

Some called for help.

Others did not move.

"Get down, Willie!"
his father shouted.
Willie dropped to the floor.
The sounds of guns and
screams grew louder.
Shells shrieked overhead.
The noise hurt Willie's ears.

After a while, the shooting ended.
Willie peeked out
the window again.
The grass was littered
with broken rifles.
Many men and horses lay still
on the ground.

The last of Lee's barefoot army
stumbled down Stage Road.
The soldiers' faces were pinched
with hunger and defeat.
Willie watched until
they were out of sight.
Was Lee giving up?

*Afternoon, April 9*

Yankees were everywhere.
They stood in front of the Court House,
talking in tight groups.
Willie glared at them from the yard.
He wouldn't let them see
that he was afraid.
But finally he went inside.

In the parlor, he found Lula
playing with her doll.
"You're not supposed
to be in here," he said.
The parlor was for company.
"Betty and me had to get away
from the noise," Lula said.
"Dolls don't have ears," Willie said.
"Betty doesn't like this war," said Lula.
"This war is the only excitement
we've had," said Willie.
He hoped that General Lee would
come back and attack again.

Out the window,
he saw his father talking
to a Confederate officer.
They walked toward
the McLean house.
Willie's mother saw them too.
"Downstairs, children," she said.

They all ran down to the kitchen.
Soon they heard boots
clumping across the porch.
Lula began to cry.
While Willie's mother
hushed her, Willie slipped
out the back door.

More Confederates
came through the gate.
A gray-bearded officer
got off a gray horse.
Willie gasped.
That must be General Lee
on Traveller, his famous horse!

Then the yard filled with
Yankee officers.
They climbed the porch steps,
led by a general with muddy boots
and a short brown beard.
Officers from both sides of the war
were meeting in Willie's house!

Willie sat on the bench
by the door.
A Yankee officer
sat down next to him.
"What's your name?" he asked.
"Wilmer McLean Junior,"
Willie replied.
"But folks just call me Willie."
"You can call me Captain Lincoln,"
the officer said.
Then he went inside.
*Lincoln!*
Could he be related
to President Lincoln?
The Yankees spoke in low tones.
Willie heard one word: *Surrender.*
But General Lee would
never give up!

Then Willie remembered
the lean faces of Lee's men,
the lame horses.
He remembered the deserter
who wanted to go home.

Just then, the door opened.

General Lee came out on the porch.

The Yankee soldiers

jumped up and saluted.

Willie held his breath.

Lee was close enough to touch.

He wore a new uniform

with a gold sash.

Gold spurs gleamed

against his shiny knee boots.

A sword hung at his side.

His brown eyes looked sad.

He walked slowly across the porch,

pulling on his gloves.

No one spoke.

The general did not look at any of them.

He gazed out over the fields

where his army waited.

Then he signaled for Traveller

and swung up on the horse's back.

The brown-bearded Union general came out.

His men followed him.

Willie realized that this man

was General Grant.

Grant raised his hat to Lee.

Lee lifted his hat in return,

then rode off toward his camp.

"Did Lee surrender?" Willie

asked Captain Lincoln.

He nodded.

"This is a great day.

Now we can go home,

and our nation can heal."

General Grant mounted

his horse and left.

Willie couldn't believe

the war was over.

It had been going on

since he was Lula's age.

And now his side had lost.

What would happen to his family?

Suddenly, blue-coated soldiers

swarmed through the gate.

They whooped and hollered.

Willie ran after them into the parlor.

His father was already there,

his face red with anger.

The soldiers were taking their furniture!

A general claimed the oval side table.

"How much?" he asked.

"It's not for sale,"

Willie's father replied.

"I mean to have it," the general said.

He held out ten dollars.

Willie's father threw

the coins on the floor.

Tables, chairs, even the inkstands
were swept out the door.
"Why are they taking our things?"
Willie asked.
"The surrender papers were signed here,"
his father answered.
"The furniture Lee and Grant
used are worth money."

Two officers began tossing
a small object back and forth.
Lula's rag doll!
She had left it behind in the parlor.
"This doll witnessed a great event,"
said a red-haired officer.
He put the toy in his pocket.
Lula flew down the hall.
"My doll!" she cried.
"Give my sister her doll!"
Willie yelled.
He ran after the officer.
He would fight to get back
Lula's doll!
But the officer mounted his horse
and rode away.
Willie looked around.
Their fence was gone.

His mother's daffodils were trampled.
Only the sofa and carpet
were left in their parlor.

"Why did they do this?"
Willie asked his father.
"Why did General Lee give up?"
"All wars must end sometime,"
his father replied.
"Lee realized it was time
to end this one."
Lula came over and put
her hand in Willie's.
"I miss Betty," she said.
Cheers rose from the Union camps.
A cannon boomed three times,
then fell silent.
Willie squeezed his sister's hand.
"Come on," he said.
"I'll help you make a new doll."

The McLean family sits on the porch of their home in the fall of 1865. The person in the back row on the right is probably Willie McLean.

# Afterword

General Robert E. Lee surrendered his army to General Ulysses S. Grant on April 9, 1865. Twenty-eight thousand shoeless, starving soldiers laid down their guns and battle flags in a mile-long procession.

But the Civil War was not over. Troops continued to fight in the West until June 2. Still, most people mark Lee's surrender as the end of a terrible war that claimed 625,000 lives.

Captain Robert Lincoln went home to Washington, D.C., after the surrender. Days later, his father, President Abraham Lincoln, was shot by John Wilkes Booth. He died on April 15.

No one knows for certain what happened to Willie McLean, the boy whose home was the site of one of the most important moments in American history. But we do know what happened to Lula's rag doll. It was taken by a Union officer named Thomas Moore. The doll stayed in the Moore family in New York for many years. In the early 1990s, the doll was returned to Appomattox Court House National Historical Park. Visitors to the park can see the doll that witnessed the end of our nation's most tragic period.

# Selected Bibliography

Calkins, Chris M. *The Battles of Appomattox Station and Appomattox Court House, April 8–9, 1865.* Lynchburg, VA: H. E. Howard, Inc., 1987.

Catton, Bruce. *A Stillness at Appomattox.* Garden City, NY: Doubleday, 1953.

Cauble, Frank P. *Biography of Wilmer McLean.* Lynchburg, VA: H. E. Howard, Inc., 1987.

Chamberlain, Joshua L. *The Passing of the Armies: An Account of the Final Campaign of the Army of the Potomac.* New York: G. P. Putnam's Sons, 1915.

Davis, Burke. *To Appomattox: Nine April Days, 1865.* New York: Rinehart and Company, 1959.

Kunhardt, Dorothy. "The Lost Rag Doll of Appomattox." *Saturday Evening Post* 223 (April 7, 1951): 174–175, 178.

Power, J. Tracy. *Lee's Miserables: Life in the Army of Northern Virginia from the Wilderness to Appomattox.* Chapel Hill, NC: University of North Carolina Press, 1998.

Trudeau, Noah Andre. *The Campaign to Appomattox.* Conshohocken, PA: Eastern National Park and Monument Association, 1995.

Wheeler, Richard. *Witness to Appomattox.* New York: Harper & Row, 1989.